## BOOKS BY JOHN GABRIEL NAVARRA

CLOCKS, CALENDARS, AND CARROUSELS

FROM GENERATION TO GENERATION

OUR NOISY WORLD

A TURTLE IN THE HOUSE

WIDE WORLD WEATHER

THE WORLD YOU INHERIT

NATURE STRIKES BACK

FLYING TODAY AND TOMORROW

DRUGS AND MAN

WHEELS FOR KIDS

SAFE MOTORBOATING FOR KIDS

# SAFE MOTORBOATING
## FOR KIDS

# SAFE MOTORBOATING FOR KIDS

## JOHN GABRIEL NAVARRA

photographs by Celeste Scala Navarra

DOUBLEDAY & COMPANY, INC., GARDEN CITY, NEW YORK

ISBN: 0-385-06512-4 TRADE
       0-385-07949-4 PREBOUND

Library of Congress Catalog Card Number 73-15090
Copyright © 1974 by John Gabriel Navarra
Printed in the United States of America
First Edition

For Johnny

# MAKE READY

Before getting under way, a boatman is quite busy. He has a checklist to go over. He makes certain, for example, that he has enough fuel on board. Running lights are turned on and checked. A good skipper even sounds his horn to make sure it is working.

The bilges are the lowest spaces within a boat's hull. A make-ready list always includes an inspection of the bilges. In addition, a good skipper opens all hatch covers. This allows engine and fuel tank spaces to ventilate. And, if he has bilge blowers, he operates them.

Hand lines and anchors are prepared for use, too. Life-saving devices are always taken out of their lockers. And the skipper places them so that they are readily available. He also makes sure that each passenger knows how to use a life vest.

In short, every good skipper is careful. He is concerned about safety. He knows his boat and uses his checklist to make sure that all equipment is operating properly. The skipper starts the engine only after he is sure that everything is in order.

# GETTING UNDER WAY

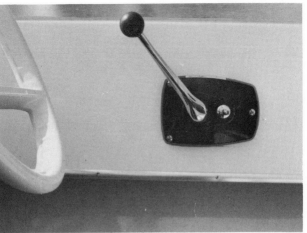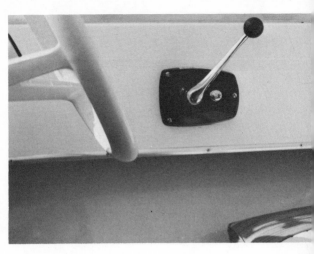

Once the engine is started, allow it to warm up. A cold engine may stall if you get under way immediately. When the engine is warm and all gauges show proper readings, cast off the mooring lines.

The single lever in the photos is used for throttle and gear shifting. When the lever is vertical, it is in the "neutral" position. This type of control is used in many electric shift outboard motors and stern drives.

When the lever is pushed from the neutral position toward the bow, it moves into forward gear. With the lever in forward gear, the boat moves ahead. Ahead means in the direction of the bow. Further advance of the lever increases the headway speed.

When the lever is pulled from the neutral position toward the stern, it moves into reverse gear. This causes the vessel to move astern. A boat that is moving astern is said to be making sternway.

# THE PROPELLER

Sailors talk about propellers a lot. The propeller is, after all, rather important. It is probably the main way the skipper has to control his boat. A sailor always refers to a propeller as if he is looking at it from one position. The sailor's view is from aft looking forward.

Propellers are made to rotate in either a clockwise or counterclockwise direction. One that turns clockwise to drive a boat forward is called a right-handed propeller. A left-handed propeller is one that turns counterclockwise to move a vessel forward.

When the control lever is pushed into forward gear, a right-handed propeller turns clockwise. This same propeller, however, turns counterclockwise when the control lever is pulled into reverse gear. Almost all single-screw boats have right-handed propellers.

A propeller is made of twisted surfaces. Sailors often refer to a propeller as a screw. But a propeller does not work its way through the water the way a screw moves through wood. A propeller blade has the shape of an airplane wing. And it works in much the same way.

When a right-handed propeller rotates clockwise, water pressure on the forward or "fat" side of the blade is reduced. As a result, the pressure on the aft side becomes greater than that on the forward side. The blade is actually pushed forward by greater pressure from the stern. And—as the propeller goes—so goes the boat!

# MARINE ENGINES

Sailors refer to engines as being either "inboard" or "outboard." An inboard engine is one that is installed within the hull. An outboard engine is mounted on the transom, that is, outboard of the hull.

All marine engines are built to do the same job. Both inboards and outboards burn a fuel to produce power. And, in each case, the power is used to turn a propeller.

Michael Long is nine years old. He is at the wheel of a boat that has an inboard engine. The engine is located in the box at the stern. When the cover is removed, we find a six-cylinder gasoline engine below.

# THE RUDDER

The barnacle-covered vertical blade shown in the photograph is called a *rudder*. It is placed directly behind the propeller. This rudder is in its amidships position. Amidships in this case means the center of the boat with reference to her length.

A rudder can be turned to the left or right of the centerline of the boat. Facing forward, a sailor refers to the left side of the boat as the port side. Starboard is the name given to the right-hand side.

Think of a boat that is making headway. This means that her propeller is rotating and she is moving forward through the water. When the rudder is turned from its amidships position, water pressure on the rudder moves the stern of the boat sideways.

A rudder operates on the principle of unequal water pressures. When a rudder is turned, one side is more exposed to the force of water flowing past it than the other side. This causes the stern to be thrust away.

When a skipper turns the wheel to change his course to starboard, the stern actually swings to port. It is the stern and not the bow that changes direction first. The stern is the only part of the boat that can be steered.

# RUDDERLESS BOATS

A boat that has an outboard mounted on the transom does not usually have a rudder. Rudderless boats are steered by turning the line of thrust of the propeller. Line of thrust means the direction in which the propeller pushes.

Maneuvering is much simpler with an outboard than with the rudder of an inboard-driven boat. But power is always needed to turn a rudderless boat. The outboard, remember, is steered by changing the direction in which the propeller pushes. This means that the propeller must be in motion in order to steer.

There is another type of rudderless boat. Sailors refer to it as an I-O drive. I-O means that the boat has an inboard engine with an outboard or stern drive.

In the photograph, the stern drive of the *Elisa* is shown. A stern drive can be tilted and lifted out of the water. This allows you to inspect and to repair an I-O propeller with ease.

The propeller of an I-O drive is powered by an inboard engine. The line of thrust of the propeller is changed by a steering arm. The rodlike steering arm of the *Elisa* can be seen in the photo. The rod is used to pivot the stern drive to port or to starboard.

# FIRES AND EXPLOSIONS

This boat was gutted by fire. The fire raged and threatened other boats that were docked at the marina. Before the fire was brought under control, the boat was completely destroyed.

There are many ways in which a fire gets started. More often than not, someone is careless. For example, a rag used to wipe up oil is left on board. Then as temperatures rise, the oil-soaked rag bursts into flame.

A rag used to soak up oil or gasoline spills is like a time bomb. When it warms up, it can burst into flames. Remove rag-bombs from the boat. Place oil-soaked rags and paper in a sealed metal container on shore.

A short circuit in the electrical system is another common way that fires start aboard boats. Become familiar with the electrical wiring on your boat. Make a habit of inspecting the wires. Be sure that the insulation on the wires is in good condition.

Large quantities of gasoline are carried on most motorboats. A gas tank can leak at any time. Gasoline vapors are heavier than air. These vapors will flow into the lowest part of the bilge spaces. Before starting an engine, always check for leaks. Ventilate all areas where gasoline vapors may accumulate.

# FIRE EXTINGUISHERS

Never spray water on a gasoline, oil, or grease fire. These materials float on water. Water will spread the area of the fire. This causes greater damage.

Carbon dioxide is a chemical that puts out gasoline, oil, and grease fires. These are the common fires on a boat. Fire extinguishers filled with carbon dioxide need to be on board every motorboat.

Fire extinguishers are classified by letter and Roman numeral. The letter indicates the type of fire the extinguisher can handle. The Roman numeral indicates the amount of chemical in the extinguisher.

A Class B extinguisher handles gasoline, oil, and grease fires. The United States Coast Guard requires motorboats to carry extinguishers that can handle Class B fires.

Make a careful survey of your boat. Then place fire extinguishers so you can get to them in an emergency. Three extinguishers are readily available to the person manning the wheel.

Mike has a B-I extinguisher. It is loaded with two pounds of dry chemical. Mike knows how to use this extinguisher.

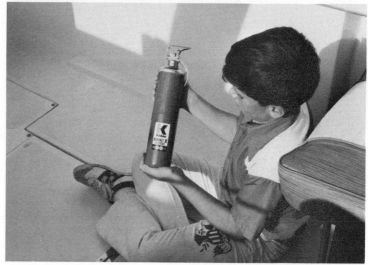

# VENTILATION

The fact that gasoline is used as a fuel creates a dangerous situation on every motorboat. Gasoline vapors are heavier than air. The heavy vapors find their way into the bilges and other closed areas.

Once gasoline vapors enter the bilges, there is no escape except through ventilation. A federal law requires a boat with an enclosed engine and fuel tank compartment to have an adequate system of ventilator ducts.

This is an intake scoop on the starboard side of the *Elisa*. It is called a *cowl*. The open part of the cowl is pointed toward the bow. As the boat moves forward, fresh air is scooped into the starboard cowl. The air flows down through a plastic duct into the engine compartment.

This is the exhaust cowl on the port side of the *Elisa*. Its opening faces the stern. Vapors from the lowest part of the engine compartment bilge are forced to the outside through this cowl.

See the ridges in the white plastic exhaust duct. This duct is on the port side of the *Elisa*. It is the passageway by which vapors in the bilge flow to the outside atmosphere. A similar duct on the starboard side carries fresh air from the outside into the bilge.

# THE CARBURETOR

The power that drives the propeller of a motorboat is produced when fuel is burned in a cylinder. A cylinder is really a combustion chamber. The *Elisa* has a six-cylinder engine. This means that there are six chambers in which fuel is burned to produce power.

Fuel is measured and sent to the cylinders by the carburetor. Combustion in the cylinder, however, depends on both air and fuel. It is the job of the carburetor to prepare the gasoline-air mixture. The mixture must have the right combination of air and fuel.

Gasoline is pumped from the fuel tank into the carburetor. As the gasoline enters the carburetor, it passes through jets with small holes. This produces a fine spray of gasoline that is then mixed with air. About fifteen pounds of air are mixed with each pound of gasoline used.

At the lower end of the carburetor there is an intake manifold. The intake manifold is a passageway that connects the carburetor with the engine's cylinders. The gasoline-air mixture prepared in the carburetor flows through the intake manifold to the cylinders.

# BACKFIRE FLAME CONTROL

At times there is a premature ignition of the gasoline-air mixture. This occurs as the mixture flows from the carburetor to the cylinders. In fact, the fuel mixture explodes in the intake manifold. The explosion is set off when the mixture comes in contact with flame from a cylinder.

The premature explosion in the intake manifold produces a flame of its own. A loud noise is also produced. The combination of flame and noise is called a *backfire*.

In order to control backfires, a device called a *flame arrestor* is used. It is secured to the air intake of the carburetor with flame-tight connections. The metallic arrestor insures that flames caused by engine backfire will be contained.

In the photograph, a rubber holder leads to the disk-shaped backfire flame arrestor. The arrestor sits on top of the carburetor. With a clean arrestor in place, there is no danger to the vessel or persons on board from backfires.

Gasoline explosions and fires on small motorboats kill a lot of people. You must be very careful when you take on fuel.

When you dock at a service station, the first thing to do is to stop all engines. Then moor the boat so it is secure. The next task is to stop any auxiliary motor, fan, or other device that might produce a spark. Also, put out all lights and galley fires.

Make sure that everyone on board understands why you are taking these precautions. Tell them they must not strike a match, smoke, or turn on any switch while you are taking on fuel.

# FUELING

Gasoline vapors are heavier than air. During fueling there is a certain amount of gasoline vapor in the air. These heavy vapors flow into the boat and seek out the lowest areas. Thus, before starting to fuel, close all hatches, ports, windows, and doors on board.

Before fueling, make an estimate of how much additional fuel the tanks will hold. This is a way of checking on the accuracy of your fuel gauge. But, in addition, this estimate helps to prevent overfilling your tanks and spilling fuel into the hull or bilges.

After completing the fueling operation, close the fill openings tightly. Wipe up any fuel that has spilled. Then open all hatches, ports, windows, and doors. Ventilate the boat for at least five minutes. Now use your nose. Check for any odor of gasoline in the engine compartment or below decks. Give special attention to the bilges.

Never fill a portable fuel tank in the boat. Remove it from the boat and place it on the fueling dock. But whether you are filling a portable or permanent tank, always keep the nozzle of the hose in contact with the fill opening. This procedure helps to guard against a possible static spark.

# LUBRICATION

The handle of the dip stick is resting on the deck in the photograph above. At the left, Mike has removed the dip stick to check the level of oil in the crankcase. It is important to maintain the oil level between the full and add marks on the dip stick.

This oil filter is a screw-on type. The filter should be replaced whenever the crankcase oil is changed.

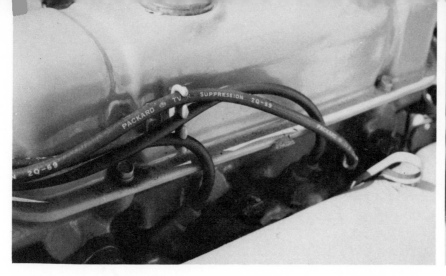
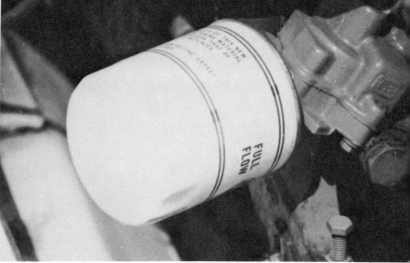

Every inboard gasoline engine has a lubrication system that places a thin film of oil on the moving parts of the engine. The coat of oil protects the moving parts from friction damage. On the *Elisa*, four quarts of oil are stored in the crankcase. Another quart of oil is stored in the filter.

The crankcase is a pan that is fastened beneath the engine. The crankcase is really a reservoir for oil. A pump forces the oil from the reservoir through channels and ducts to all the moving parts of the engine.

In an outboard engine there is no oil reservoir. The oil is mixed with the gasoline. Remember, gasoline is more volatile than oil. Oil droplets remain and condense on the metallic surfaces when the gasoline is vaporized. New oil is constantly supplied to the moving parts of the outboard motor so no filter is needed.

# COOLING SYSTEMS

Marine engines—inboard and outboard—generate a lot of heat. The explosion of the gasoline-air mixture in a cylinder produces temperatures of 1,500° to 4,500° F. The metal parts of the engine must be cooled or trouble will develop.

Water is the agent that is commonly used to cool marine engines. In most cases, raw seawater is pumped aboard. The cool seawater passes through the engine water jackets to draw off the heat from the hot engine.

Some large boats use closed fresh-water cooling systems. These systems are similar to those used to cool automobile engines. There is one difference, however. After the fresh water is circulated through the marine engine, it passes through a keel cooler rather than an air-cooled radiator.

A keel cooler is a type of radiator. It is mounted outside on the hull of the boat. Seawater passes over the keel cooler as the boat moves through the water. The cool seawater removes the heat carried by the fresh water inside the keel cooler.

On some large boats a heat exchanger, mounted inside the hull, is used instead of a keel cooler. In this system, seawater is taken on board and pumped into the heat exchanger. The cool seawater passes over the coils of the closed fresh-water system to remove the heat. Then the hot seawater is pumped overboard.

Study the action photograph of this stern drive. The photo was taken while the boat was making headway. The starboard side of the drive unit is located in the lower part of the photo. Can you see the fine stream of water that is being discharged from the starboard side? This is seawater that was drawn into the engine to cool it.

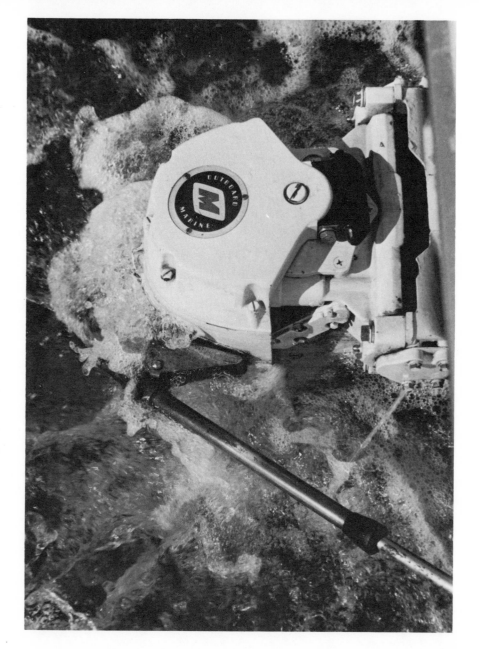

# ELECTRICAL SYSTEMS

Every gasoline engine needs an electrical source to fire the spark plugs. Remember, it is a spark from the spark plug that ignites the fuel-air mixture in the cylinder.

Inboard engines have a battery ignition system. A battery feeds twelve volts of electricity to a coil. The coil increases the voltage to as much as twenty thousand volts. Then the coil sends the high-voltage electricity to a distributor. It is the distributor's job to send the high-voltage current to the spark plugs.

The coil is in the lower right of the photo. A single wire leads from the top of the coil to the center of the distributor cap. Six wires lead away from the top of the distributor. Count them. Each wire leads to a spark plug. This is a six-cylinder engine.

A two-cylinder outboard motor uses a magneto to generate the high voltage needed for its spark plugs. A magneto is a small electric generator. It uses the magnetic field of permanent magnets to generate high-voltage pulses. The rotating motion of the motor's flywheel operates the magneto.

Large outboard motors, however, use a battery ignition system to generate the high-voltage current that is needed. In this way, large outboards are similar to inboard engines.

A battery constantly supplies energy to spark plugs and electrical equipment. Thus it needs to be recharged. An alternator—an electric generator—is used to charge the battery. In the photo, you see an alternator with its pulley. A belt from the engine crankshaft drives the alternator.

# PUMPING THE BILGES

When a boat is making headway, water—often as spray—finds its way aboard. But water, in whatever way it comes aboard, works its way into the bilges. In order to keep a boat dry and safe, you need a way to clear the bilges of water.

The rectangular pump at the left is in the bilge of the *Elisa*. Water that collects in the bilge is pumped up through tubing to a thru-hull fitting. The tubing with its thru-hull fitting on the port side of the *Elisa* is shown in the upper photo on this page.

# RUNNING LIGHTS

The light carried on the bow of this boat is called a *combined lantern*. It shows a green light to starboard and a red light to port.

Special running lights are carried on a motorboat. They are used for identification and warning. These lights must be shown from sunset to sunrise when under way. The arc through which they can be seen is called out in points. One point is equal to an arc of $11\frac{1}{4}°$.

On inland waters, western rivers, and the Great Lakes, a motorboat under 26 feet in length shows a combined lantern on the bow. The lights in the lantern are 10-point lights. This means that the green light can be seen from dead ahead through an arc of $112\frac{1}{2}°$ to starboard. The red light shows through a similar arc, but on the port side. In addition, a 32-point white light is carried on the stern. Since 32 points is equal to 360°, the stern light can be seen all around the horizon.

Another scheme of lights is required on the high seas and off-shore coastal waters. Motorboats under 40 feet in length have a combined lantern on the bow. The lantern shows a 10-point green light to starboard and a 10-point red light to port. At the stern a 12-point white light is shown. The stern light shows through an arc of 135°. The midpoint of its arc is seen from dead astern of the vessel. Between the stern light and the combined lantern on the bow there is a white light of 20 points. The 20-point white light is carried at least 3 feet higher than the colored lights. The arc of the 20-point light is 225°. Its midpoint is fixed to shine dead ahead.

The running lights of the *Elisa* are rigged for the international rules used on the high seas. These lights may also be used on inland waters, western rivers, and the Great Lakes. The staff holding the 20-point white light of the *Elisa* can be seen in the photograph.

# WHISTLES AND BELLS

The term "motorboat" means any vessel 65 feet in length or less that is propelled by an engine. Motorboats are classified according to length as Class A, 1, 2, or 3.

A boat that is less than 16 feet in length is placed in Class A. Class 1 motorboats run from 16 to less than 26 feet in length. A Class 2 boat may have a length from 26 to 40 feet. Class 3 boats run from 40 to not more than 65 feet in length.

A whistle or horn is needed to sound passing signals and fog signals. Boats in Class 1, 2, and 3 must carry a whistle or horn. On Class 2 and Class 3 boats, a bell is needed, too. The bell is used when these boats are at anchor in a fog.

Basically, there are three situations that may lead to a collision at sea. These occur when a boat meets, crosses, or overtakes another that is under way.

There is a set of uniform rules for preventing collisions. When you are at the wheel of a boat, other skippers have the right to assume you know the rules. Turn the page to learn how the rules work.

This sailboat approached from starboard. It is now crossing our course. You must keep out of the way of any boat approaching from the right in the arc of your ten-point green light. The signal for this situation is one blast of the horn. We can either slow down or turn out of the boat's way to our starboard.

We are approaching these boats head to head. Neither we nor they have the right-of-way. In this situation, each vessel must give one blast on the horn and alter course to starboard. After one blast, we will swing to the right. The other vessels will pass us on our port side.

This boat is overtaking us. We have the right-of-way. The overtaking boat has given two blasts on her horn. This means that she is going to pass and keep us on her starboard side. If she wished to pass and keep us on her port side, she would have given one blast on her horn.

This boat is returning from sea. We are heading out to sea. Since we wish to hold our course, we give two blasts on our horn. The two blasts mean that we are going to hold her on our starboard side. If this vessel was on our port side, one blast would say we are holding course.

# SAFETY FIRST

One U. S. Coast Guard-approved life-saving device must be available for every person on board. But remember: A life-saving device is effective only when properly used.

Mike slips into his buoyant vest before the boat gets under way. There are ties and straps that must be adjusted. Mike makes sure that his vest fits snugly, with all ties and fasteners pulled taut.

It is a good practice to have a ring buoy on board, too. One of your passengers may fall overboard. A ring buoy fitted with a grab rope and sixty feet of line is the best way to help such a person. The ring buoy can be used to pull the person back to the boat.

Never go barefoot. A foot without protection is easily stubbed and cut. Bare feet and a wet deck are a dangerous combination. Always wear sneakers that have skidproof bottoms.

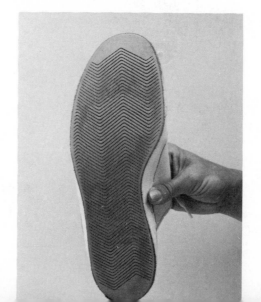

# TIDES AND LINES

A stern spring line is made fast to a cleat. This cleat is located on the port side of the *Elisa*. The pole to which the end of the spring line is fixed is at the right of the photo.

Lines that are used to tie a boat to a dock are called *mooring lines*. The bow line and the stern line are the two mooring lines most often used. A bow line runs forward from a cleat on the bow to the dock where it is made fast. A stern line runs aft from the stern to the dock.

Sometimes breast lines are used. A breast line may run from the bow or the stern to the dock. A breast line is fixed so it runs perpendicular from the boat to the dock. Such a line prevents sideways movement.

A spring line is used to limit the fore-and-aft movement of the boat. A stern spring line runs from a stern cleat forward to the dock. A bow spring runs aft from a bow cleat to the dock.

A boatman on a lake does not worry about tides when securing to a dock. In a tidal area, however, the water at dockside may drop six feet from its high-tide to its low-tide level. Lines in a tidal area must be carefully set with enough slack. The slack allows the boat to rise and fall with the tide.

# THE ANCHOR

Every boat should carry at least two anchors. One anchor may be small and lightweight. It is used when anchoring for a short time in a protected area. The second anchor should be heavier and larger than the first. The heavier anchor is used when anchoring overnight. It is also used when water conditions indicate that the lighter anchor might drag and not hold.

There are many types of anchors. The anchor shown in the photo is a Danforth anchor. It has twin flukes that pivot at the lower end of a long shank. The upper end of the shank seen at the left of the photo is lashed to the deck. The stock—with rubber tips at either end—is attached to the rear of the flukes. The flukes cut into the sea bottom and give an anchor its holding power.

A rubber-coated chain is attached to the upper end of the shank. A line is attached to the other end of the chain. The combination of anchor line and chain is called a *rode*.

In the photo, the anchor line goes through a deck opening to a locker below decks. The area in which the anchor line is stored is called the anchor locker. The inboard end of the anchor line is made fast to a bitt in the locker. A bitt is a piece of iron or timber that is securely fastened.

The length of the anchor rode that is placed in the water is called the *scope*. A scope equal to seven times the depth of the water is the best for anchoring. This means that if the water depth is five feet, you should put out a scope equal to thirty-five feet.

With a good scope, the heavy chain attached to the anchor shank will lie along the bottom. Thus the pull of the rode on the shank will be as near to horizontal as possible. This kind of pull helps the flukes to dig in and hold.

# CHARTS

Mike plots a course on his chart. Then he uses his compass to steer the course. The compass shows that Mike is moving on a heading of 105°.

The four main points of a compass are called *cardinal points*. North, east, south, and west are the cardinal points. Northeast, southeast, southwest, and northwest are the points between the main points.

A chart is an important item of equipment. You should carry up-to-date charts for the waters you are cruising. A chart shows the depths of water, locations of obstructions, and the adjacent land.

Mike is studying a chart of the Manasquan River. The safe-boating channel is clearly marked. Water depths outside the channel are only one and two feet. From the chart Mike learns the number of each buoy that marks the channel he must follow.

# AIDS TO NAVIGATION

The waters of the United States are marked for safe navigation by a system of buoys. This conical-shaped buoy is called a *nun*. It is red and marks the right side of the channel as you move from the sea and head up a river. Nuns are given even numbers. The numbers increase from seaward. This nun is about four miles from the mouth of the river.

This cylindrical-shaped buoy is called a *can*. Cans are given odd numbers and are painted black. Black cans mark the left side of the channel as you enter from the sea. Of course, if you reverse your direction the scheme is reversed, too. Cans mark the right side and nuns mark the left side of the channel as you head downriver toward the sea.

Make a study of local buoys. Each buoy marks a definite spot. A buoy that you observe can be used to locate your position on a local chart.

Most buoys serve as day-marks. Some buoys also carry lights and are used for navigation at night. Red lights are used on red buoys. Green lights are used on black buoys. Your local chart shows the location of lighted buoys and other aids to navigation.

In the photo, the single pile light has a square daymark. This is another type of aid to navigation. The daymark is black with an odd number. It serves in place of a can, and so its light is green.

A single pile light that takes the place of a nun carries a red light. Its daymark is a red triangle with an even number.

# THE WEATHER

Always check the existing weather and sea conditions before getting under way. Then make sure that you have the latest forecast for your area. When warnings are in effect, don't go out!

Even on the best of days, watch for any change while afloat. At the first sign of threatening weather, seek shelter. For example, be alert for the approach of dark, threatening clouds. Such clouds may bring a sudden squall or thunderstorm.

Always beware of any steady increase in the wind or the sea. An increase in wind velocity that is opposite in direction to a strong tidal current is a special danger. Rip tides can develop when wind and current move in opposite directions. The steep waves of a rip tide can cause you to lose control of your boat. You can capsize in a rough sea.

A small-craft warning—one red pennant—is flying at the U. S. Coast Guard station at Point Pleasant, New Jersey. Wind speeds up to thirty-eight miles per hour have been clocked. Under these conditions, even the inland waters are very rough. Swells and waves in the open sea are running greater than ten feet.

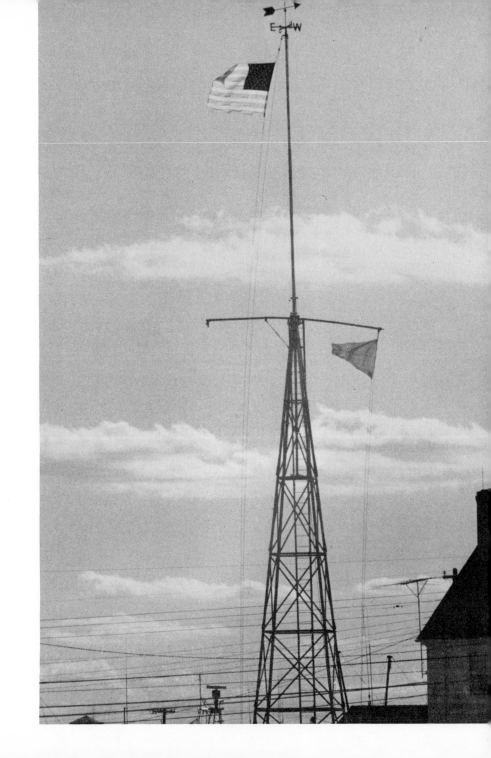

The waters of the Manasquan are at high tide. It is at least three feet from the deck to the surface of the water. The dock stands well above the high-tide level. Cumulus clouds are in the sky. It is a beautiful day.

Rain and gale-force winds have made the waters of the river rise. The deck of the dock is awash with water. The water level stands three feet above the normal high-tide level. A sheet of stratus clouds is drawn across the sky.

# COASTAL WARNING DISPLAYS

A simple system of visual signals warns a sailor of dangerous weather conditions. Four separate signals are used. Pennants and flags are displayed for the daytime signals. Red and white lights are used for nighttime signals.

*Small-craft warning:* One red pennant is shown by day. A red light above a white light is displayed at night. These signals mean that a sailor can expect wind speeds up to thirty-eight miles per hour.

*Gale warning:* Two red pennants are displayed by day. A white light above a red light is shown at night. When a sailor sees these signals he knows that high winds—39 to 54 miles per hour—will whip the surface of the sea.

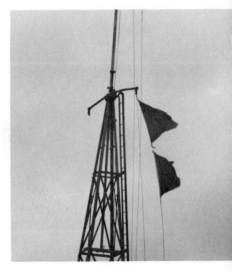

*Storm warning:* A single square red flag with a black center is flown by day. Two red lights are shown at night. These signals mean that wind speeds will go above fifty-five miles per hour.

*Hurricane warning:* Two square red flags with black centers are displayed by day. A white light between two red lights is the night-time signal. These signals mean real trouble. A tropical cyclone has wind speeds of seventy-four miles per hour and above.

Each day brings a new experience when you are boating. And each day you learn something. One of the first things you find out about boating is that the work is never done. Before starting out, you must "make ready." While under way, you have many things to observe and "tasks that need doing." Then when you return you must "secure" the boat and "wash it down." If you think it's fun and worth it all, you are a true sailor!

# A NAUTICAL DICTIONARY

*abaft.* Toward the stern.

*abeam.* In a direction at right angles from the center of the vessel.

*about.* To go in the opposite direction.

*abreast.* Side by side.

*aft.* Near the stern.

*ahead.* In the direction of the boat's bow.

*amidships.* In the center of the boat.

*astern.* In the direction of the stern.

*avast.* To stop.

*aye.* Yes.

*beam.* The breadth of a vessel at its widest point.

*bearing.* The direction of an object from the boat.

*belay.* To make a line fast by taking turns around a cleat.

*below.* Under the deck.

*berth.* The place where a boat lies.

*bilge.* That part of the floor of the boat upon which she would rest if aground.

*bow.* The forward part of a boat.

*broadside.* The whole side of a boat.

*bunk.* Bed on board ship.

*burgee.* A small flag, either pointed or swallowtail.

*capsize.* To overturn.

*cardinal points.* The four main points of the compass.

*chock.* A deck fitting through which lines are passed. A wedge used to secure something.

*cleat.* An anvil-shaped fitting used to belay ropes to.

*close aboard.* Alongside, close to the hull.

*coil.* To lay a rope up in a circle.

*deck.* The planked floor of a boat.

*draft.* The vertical distance from the waterline to the lowest part of the vessel beneath the water.

*ebb.* The flow of the tide away from the shore.

*ensign.* The flag carried by a ship to show her nationality.

*fathom.* Six feet.

*flukes.* Broad triangular plates on an anchor.

*fore.* Used to identify things forward of amidships.

*founder.* When a boat fills with water and sinks.

*freeboard.* The vertical distance from the waterline to the gunwale.

*galley.*  The place where the cooking is done.

*gangway.*  Where people pass in and out of a boat.

*gunwale.*  The top edge of the hull.

*head.*  A toilet compartment.

*heave-to.*  To put a vessel in the position of lying-to.

*helm.*  The machinery by which a vessel is steered.

*hold.*  The interior of a vessel where cargo is stored.

*hull.*  The body of a vessel.

*keel.*  The lowest framing timber of a vessel that runs fore-and-aft.

*kink.*  A twist in a line.

*knot.*  A unit of speed equal to one nautical mile per hour.

*ladder.*  Stairs aboard a vessel.

*lee.*  The side opposite to that from which the wind blows.

*leeward.*  In a direction opposite to that from which the wind blows.

*line.*  Rope that has been put to use.

*mile.*  A nautical mile is generally equal to 6,080 feet.

*nip.*  A short turn in a rope.

*part.*  To break a rope.

*port.*  The left side of a boat as you look forward.

*quarter.*  The part of a vessel's side between midships and the stern.

*round in.*  To haul in on a rope.

*rudder.*  An underwater vertical blade that can be pivoted to steer the vessel.

*sea.*  Waves caused by wind blowing at the time.

*slack.*  The part of a rope that hangs down loose.

*slip.*  To let go.

*splice.*  To join two ropes together by interweaving their strands.

*spray.*  Water dashed from the top of a wave by wind.

*starboard.*  The right side of a vessel looking forward.

*stern.*  The after end of a boat.

*strike.*  To lower a flag.

*swab.*  A mop.

*taut.*  Tight or snug.

*transom.*  Planking across the stern of a boat.

*wake.*  The track a vessel leaves behind when making headway.

*way.*  Movement of a boat through the water.

*windward.*  The direction from which the wind blows.

JOHN GABRIEL NAVARRA, the author of *Safe Motorboating for Kids,* is professor of geoscience and was, for ten years, chairman of the division of science at Jersey City State College. As both a teacher and a writer, Dr. Navarra has an international reputation. He was the teacher of the first televised science course to be offered in the South when he was on the faculty of East Carolina University. He has written a number of trade books for young readers as well as adult science books, and is the senior author of a complete series of science textbooks, grades kindergarten through nine, that are used by millions of schoolchildren throughout the United States. Dr. Navarra's experience as vice commander of a flotilla in the United States Coast Guard Auxiliary gives him broad personal knowledge of seamanship.

CELESTE SCALA NAVARRA has traveled all over the world with her husband taking photographs for his books. Mrs. Navarra participates in the conferences that lead to the development of the idea for each book and then suggests ways for the book to be brought to life visually. She feels that each project has its own challenge. There is always the task of researching the topic. But for Mrs. Navarra the most important part is finding the right subject for her camera.